Energy Policy: Errors, Illusions and Market Realities

COLIN ROBINSON

IEA
Institute of Economic Affairs
1993

First published in October 1993

by

THE INSTITUTE OF ECONOMIC AFFAIRS

2 Lord North Street, Westminster, London SW1P 3LB

© The Institute of Economic Affairs 1993

Occasional Paper No. 90

All rights reserved

ISSN 0073-909X

ISBN 0-255 36326-5

Printed in Great Britain by

GORON PRO-PRINT CO LTD, LANCING, WEST SUSSEX

Set in Plantin 11 on 13 point

Contents

Foreword

A PERENNIAL CONCEIT of governments is that well-intentioned politicians and their willing allies in the Civil Service can often produce better results for the community than unaided market forces. As Professor Colin Robinson puts it, the belief is that 'wise and enlightened people, acting in the general interest, ought to be able to do better'. This *IEA Occasional Paper* is a powerful demonstration of this fallacy in the context of the UK energy industries since the Second World War. Most developments in 'fuel policy' can be attributed to the self-interest of pressure groups, or to planners' ability to create self-fulfilling prophecies. Even privatisation, in gas and electricity, whose principal effect is to distance government from the markets concerned, and thus lessen the scope for government failure, has not yet resulted in freeing markets. Indeed, the attempt to privatise coal, he argues, is even now prolonging the escape from government failure.

The 'reverse invisible hand' of political and bureaucratic intervention, well-intentioned as it may be, ends in surrender to the interests of the more powerful industry pressure groups. Fortunately, this 'invisible hand' is itself prone to divisions, as in the conflicts which emerge between the Treasury's need to raise revenues, and the sponsoring Departments. But it is by good fortune rather than intention that the outcome benefits the general welfare.

The general theme, of government failure, is one which has frequently been voiced in IEA publications. But Professor Robinson, very interestingly, does not only demonstrate, in the thorough manner to be expected of one so well-versed in fuel economics, how perverse 'fuel policy' has been. He considers carefully the possibility that 'wise and enlightened people' *could* do better.

[7]

In doing this, while giving them due weight, he departs both from the neo-classical refutation of intervention in markets and the public choice theorists, in that he gives pride of place to Austrian perspectives on markets – that of being, on the one hand, a discovery mechanism in which consumers' needs can be articulated and, on the other, a profit-oriented process in which attacks, direct or indirect, on established positions can be mounted. Some challenging ideas emerge from this – for example, that regulators should not aim to simulate 'perfectly competitive' outcomes, and that they are as prone to failure as the governments that created them.

> 'Regulators can never know what the outcome of a competitive market would have been, so providing them with tighter rules or co-ordinating the actions of one regulator with those of other regulators cannot help decision-making though it may well make it more rigid.' (p.55)

Professor Robinson gives short shrift to the usual economic excuses for intervening in fuel markets, in particular: supply will not be physically more 'secure'; the balance of payments will not be improved; there is little merit in supporting indigenous fuels as a hedge against world price movements; and to assert that markets are prone to 'short-termism' neglects the more plausible 'short-termism' of politicians. Again, environmental concerns will be better met by clarification of property rights than by relying on political action, always likely to be polluted by interests dressed in green clothes.

So Professor Robinson uses his expertise in the political economy of energy industries to give an unusually thorough review of the case for extending market forces at the expense of government action. One of the abiding problems in establishing the credibility of economists in real governmental or business decisions is that their predominantly neo-classical training both encourages the idea of playing God in the machine and diverts them from studying how markets develop, not least in response to attempts to coerce them.

Professor Robinson's Austrian counterblast should make even the most convinced economic do-gooder think again.

The views expressed in this paper are those of the author, not of the Institute (which has no corporate view), its Trustees, Directors or Advisers. It is published by the Institute as a contribution to public debate about energy policy.

October 1993   MICHAEL BEESLEY
Managing Trustee, Institute of Economic Affairs;
Professor of Economics, Emeritus, London Business School

Acknowledgements

This *IEA Occasional Paper* is a much expanded version of a lecture given at the British Institute of Energy Economics on 15 June 1993 in response to the Institute's award of the title of 'Energy Economist of the Year'. I am grateful for helpful comments on a draft of the paper by four referees. Responsibility for any remaining errors is, of course, mine alone.

October 1993   C.R.

The Author

COLIN ROBINSON was educated at the University of Manchester, and then worked for 11 years as a business economist before being appointed to the chair of Economics at the University of Surrey in 1968. He has been a member of the Electricity Supply Research Council and of the Secretary of State for Energy's Advisory Council for Research and Development in Fuel and Power (ACORD), and is currently on the electricity panel of the Monopolies and Mergers Commission.

Professor Robinson has written widely on energy including, for the IEA, *A Policy for Fuel?* (IEA Occasional Paper No.31, 1969); *Competition for Fuel* (Supplement to Occasional Paper No.31, 1971); *The Energy 'Crisis' and British Coal* (IEA Hobart Paper No.59, 1974); (with Eileen Marshall) *What Future for British Coal?* (IEA Hobart Paper No.89, 1981), and *Can Coal Be Saved?* (IEA Hobart Paper No.105, 1985); *Competition in Electricity? The Government's Proposals for Privatising Electricity Supply* (IEA Inquiry No.2, March 1988); *Making a Market in Energy* (IEA Current Controversies No.3, December 1992); and he contributed a paper, 'Privatising the Energy Industries', to *Privatisation & Competition* (IEA Hobart Paperback No.28, 1989).

Professor Robinson became a member of the IEA's Advisory Council in 1982 and was appointed its Editorial Director in 1992. He was appointed a Trustee of the Wincott Foundation in 1993. He received the British Institute of Energy Economics' award as 'Economist of the Year 1992'.

Energy Policy:
Errors, Illusions and Market Realities
COLIN ROBINSON

1. Was There a Policy?

IN A PAPER about British energy policy, written in 1969,[1] I investigated government actions in the British energy market in the 1950s and 1960s. One of the main conclusions was that the process of 'policy' formation seemed quite different from the approach which government planners are popularly supposed to adopt, which is:

o make a forecast on 'unchanged policy' assumptions;

o formulate 'national interest' objectives which will produce a more desirable outcome than if there were no change in policy;

o find instruments capable of achieving those objectives;

o use the chosen means to attain the selected objectives.

Had such an approach been pursued, one would be able to identify studies (internal to the civil service or published) which had led to particular actions in the energy market. But no such studies appear to exist. In practice, 'policies' were instant responses to apparently pressing problems in the energy field which seemed likely to be of concern to the electorate and which were therefore capable of swaying votes. Typically, the government of the day reacted to each new problem with a short-term political 'fix'. But though the fix was directed at the immediate political impact of whatever

---

[1] Colin Robinson, *A Policy for Fuel?*, Occasional Paper 31, London: IEA, 1969, and *Competition for Fuel*, Supplement to Occasional Paper 31, IEA, 1971.

awkward problem had arisen, its effects in the market could not be confined to the short run. Inevitably, there would be long-term consequences. Inevitably too, those consequences would either be unforeseen or else, if they were to some extent predicted, they would be ignored because immediate political issues seemed so overwhelmingly important.

Haphazard Policy

Energy 'policy' therefore consisted of a ' haphazard process of piling measure on measure'.[2] That conclusion will, of course, surprise no-one who has studied government policies in other fields. Given the impossibility of providing sufficiently accurate central forecasts and specifying the 'national interest', and given that politicians have little incentive to act in the general interest, government industrial policies are normally dominated by short-term political considerations. However, the nature of the 'policy' formation process, in energy as elsewhere, could not be admitted. Governments did not say that they were taking *ad hoc* action designed principally to capture votes. Instead, actions were justified in the language of welfare economics. Periodically, the set of short-term 'fixes' which happened to exist at the time would be gathered together in a White Paper (such as those of 1965 and 1967)[3] or a Ministerial speech, described as though it were some analytically-sound, coherent whole designed to deal with failures in markets and dignified by the title of 'policy'.

Increasing Intervention

A related issue, arising from the haphazard process of policy formulation, seemed (in 1969) at first sight paradoxical. On grounds of principle, it appeared difficult to make a case for a specific policy for energy. Nevertheless, government action in the energy market increased over time as though there were a ratchet effect similar to that which, it has been argued, applies

---

2   Robinson, *A Policy for Fuel?*, *op. cit.*, p.18.

3   *Fuel Policy*, Cmnd. 2798, London: HMSO, 1965, and *Fuel Policy*, Cmnd. 3438, London: HMSO, 1967.

to government activity in general. Most government intervention in energy markets appeared unsuccessful, even in achieving its own specified objectives. But failure was no deterrent. The authorities always concluded that they had intervened in the wrong way rather than that they should have taken no action at all; moreover, unsuccessful government action generated unintended side-effects which provided new excuses for intervention to counteract the effects of the original measures. There seemed to be a 'law of increasing intervention' which meant that, over the years, a substantial protective wall was erected which seemed '...out of all proportion to the problems involved'.[4]

The Power of Pressure Groups

My 1969 paper, however, failed to emphasise sufficiently one very significant determinant of government action in energy markets. Though 'policy' consisted of a series of short-term fixes, it took place against a background of constant powerful pressure from producer interest groups. The actions of these pressure groups were the source of the long-term upward trend in government activity in energy markets, resulting in increasing intervention and imparting a protectionist slant to government action.

This *Occasional Paper* re-examines the case for an energy policy, discussing how government action in the energy field has evolved and considering what justification there might be for a specific policy towards energy. It starts in Sections 2 and 3 with a brief overview of British policy towards the energy industries in the post-war period as a whole[5] which is intended to expose the general drift of government action and to

---

4   Robinson, *A Policy for Fuel?*, *op. cit.*, p.25.

5   For more detailed historical accounts, see William G. Shepherd, *Economic Performance under Public Ownership - British Fuel and Power*, Yale University Press, 1965; PEP, *A Fuel Policy for Britain*, 1966; Colin Robinson, 'Die Energiewirtschaft in Grossbritannien: Entwicklung under Perspektiven', *Zeitschrift für Energie Wirtschaft*, 2/91, 1991, and 'Energy Trends and the Development of Energy Policy in the United Kingdom', *Surrey Energy Economics Centre Discussion Paper No.61*, February 1992.

explain why it followed the course it did. Section 4 then summarises the conclusions that can be drawn from post-war experience of energy policy, and Section 5 addresses the question of whether or not a case can be made for a government energy policy.

2. Energy 'Policies' Over the Post-War Years

IDENTIFYING WHAT CONSTITUTES 'energy policy' in Britain and how it has changed over the years is not straightforward since, as explained above, governments have not had clearly defined policies towards the energy industries. At times – as in the mid-1960s – there was a fashion for issuing White Papers which set out what the government of the day claimed to be its policy. At other times, even though White Papers were absent, many measures taken by governments - taxes, subsidies, direct controls and attempts to influence the actions of state and private corporations - had significant effects on the energy market. Indeed, since three of the energy industries (coal, gas and electricity) were nationalised for most of the post-war years and since governments set financial targets and intervened extensively in the pricing and investment decisions of all the nationalised industries,[6] it is obvious that governments were one of the main forces attempting to shape events in the British energy market.

Three sub-periods can usefully be distinguished in considering the evolution of government action in energy markets since the Second World War: the 25 years or so from the end of the War to the late 1960s and the subsequent period of about 15 years up to the mid-1980s; these sub-periods are discussed below. Section 3 then considers the last eight years.

---

6 A good discussion of government policy towards the nationalised industries up to 1979 is in David Heald, 'The Economic and Financial Control of UK Nationalised Industries', *The Economic Journal*, June 1980, pp. 243-65.

From 1945 to the Late 1960s:
Protecting British Coal and Promoting Nuclear Power

Protecting Coal

The constant element in British government policy towards the fuel industries in the post-war period is protection for the nationalised British coal industry.[7] Coal protection originated in the early post-war years when planning was in vogue, following Britain's wartime experiences. Coal accounted for almost 90 per cent of fuel consumption in 1950 and virtually the whole of indigenous fuel production (Table 1).At the time it appeared the only likely source of large energy supplies for the British economy. The Labour government of the day, closely allied with the miners and concerned both about the balance of payments and about energy security, was anxious to avoid dependence on imported coal.

The British coal industry had been starved of resources during the war: production had fallen from about 230 million tonnes in 1938 to only 187 million tonnes in 1945.[8] Energy policy in the early post-war period consisted of efforts to expand the industry and, for a few years, those efforts had some success. By 1952 production of deep-mined and open-cast coal had regained its pre-war level of 230 million tonnes. But that proved to be the post-war peak of British coal output (Figure 1).

Consumers Turning Away...

Despite the efforts of the planners, consumers were beginning to turn away from coal towards oil as the relative price of coal increased. British deep-mined coal was a labour-intensive

---

7   Robinson, *A Policy for Fuel?* and *Competition for Fuel, op. cit.*; Colin Robinson and Eileen Marshall, *What Future for British Coal?*, Hobart Paper No.89, London: IEA, 1981, and *Can Coal Be Saved?*, Hobart Paper No. 105, IEA, 1985; and Colin Robinson, 'Coal Liberalisation: Retrospect and Prospect', in Peter Pearson (ed.), *Prospects for British Coal*, London: Macmillan, 1991.

8   Statistics on coalmining and other energy industries are in *Digest of UK Energy Statistics* (annual), Department of Trade and Industry, and its predecessors such as the *Ministry of Power Statistical Digest*.

Table 1:
United Kingdom Fuel Production and Consumption, 1950-1993

	1950		1960		1973		1985		1993*	
	mtce	% of total	mtce	% of total	mtce	% of total	mtce	% of total	mtce	% of total
PRODUCTION										
Coal	219	100	198	99	132	70	94	24	55	16
Oil	–	–	–	–	1	1	217	54	162	48
Hydro	1	–	2	1	2	1	2	1	2	1
Nuclear	–	–	1	–	10	5	22	5	31	9
Natural Gas	–	–	–	–	43	23	63	16	89	26
TOTAL	220	100	201	100	188	100	398	100	339	100
CONSUMPTION[1]										
Coal	208	87	199	70	133	35	105	30	80	22
Oil	30	13	84	29	193	50	134	39	140	39
Hydro	1	–	2	1	2	1	2	1	2	1
Nuclear	–	–	1	–	10	3	22	6	31	9
Natural Gas	–	–	–	–	44	11	82	24	95	27
Imported Electricity[2]	–	–	–	–	–	–	–	–	7	2
TOTAL	239	100	286	100	382	100	345	100	355	100

[1] Home consumption, including non-energy uses and bunker fuel.
[2] from France
– means less than 0·5 mtce or less than 0·5%.
* estimated
mtce means million tonnes coal equivalent.

Sources: Department of Trade and Industry, *Digests of UK Energy Statistics, Energy Trends.*

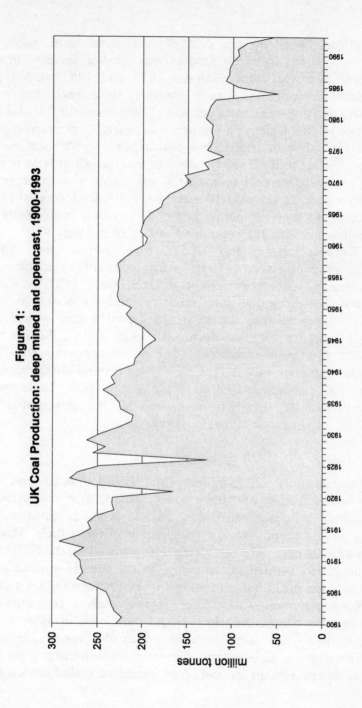

Figure 1:
UK Coal Production: deep mined and opencast, 1900-1993

industry (over 60 per cent of total costs were wages or wage-related) in which productivity failed to increase in the early post-war years. Between 1950 and 1957 output per manshift remained virtually constant: since wages increased substantially, wage costs per unit of output rose and so did the price of coal which, on average, was nearly 75 per cent higher in 1957 than in 1950. Thus coal began to price itself out of the market and oil sales started to increase sharply as it was substituted for coal in industry and across a wide range of other uses. In the next 10 years, total oil sales increased at an annual average compound rate of 11 per cent and sales of oil to industry rose at a compound rate of 14 per cent.

Between 1952 and 1957, coal output and home consumption of coal were fairly constant at a time of increasing energy consumption. But, from 1957 onwards, even though by that time labour productivity in deep mining had begun to rise, unsold stocks mounted and output and consumption went into decline. In 1960, coal production was only 198 million tonnes and coal consumption was 199 million tonnes (Table 1). Coal's share of total energy slipped from 87 per cent in 1950 to 70 per cent in 1960. Employment in the industry (nearly three-quarters of a million just after the War) also began to drop after 1957.

Political Influence...

At this time, the National Coal Board (NCB) and the National Union of Mineworkers (NUM) had considerable political influence which they used to persuade governments to protect them from the competition of other fuels. That is not to say they were completely successful. Both the NCB and the NUM wanted governments to commit themselves to a minimum coal production target of 200 million tonnes a year. No government was willing to make such a commitment, given the huge costs which would have been likely as taxes, subsidies or administrative controls were applied. Nevertheless, Labour and Conservative administrations did provide protection for coal on an increasing scale from the late

1950s onwards in an attempt to moderate the rate at which output and employment were falling.

...and the Views of Politicians

Politicians were for many years unwilling to state openly what they must surely have recognised – that coal, at the time Britain's only large indigenous source of fuel, had resumed the decline which had begun after the First World War and that government's ability to arrest that decline was very limited. They had no plan for coal though they would dearly have liked to avoid facing the problems which the industry brought them and for which, since it was nationalised, they supposedly carried responsibility.

Governments acted in a series of instant responses to coal industry problems which, in the 1950s and 1960s, appeared urgent. They changed their 'policies' as the problems appeared to change even though that caused inconsistencies. In 1954 the government encouraged the use of oil in power stations because there was believed to be a coal 'shortage'; by the late 1950s they reversed that policy because of the perception that by then a 'surplus' of coal existed; also in the late 1950s, as coal stocks built up, the government imposed restrictions on coal imports which then, in one form or another, persisted for the next 30 years.

Even if Ministers had known how to formulate and implement an explicit fuel policy, they would probably have felt that the publication of such a policy - which would inevitably have contained forecasts of continued decline in coal - would have caused them serious embarrassment. It was not until publication of two White Papers on *Fuel Policy*, one in 1965 and the other in 1967,[9] that any effort was made to justify the efforts to protect coal which by then were about 10 years' old.

---

9   Cmnd. 2798 and Cmnd. 3438 respectively, *op. cit.*

The two White Papers in effect concluded that Britain just happened to have achieved the right policy for fuel. Given the process of 'policy' formulation, it would have been a miracle if that had been true. The papers simply provided *ex post* justifications for the haphazard collection of measures affecting the fuel industries which had accumulated since the late 1950s. Neither took a new look at policy. The principal instrument which affected the terms of competition among the fuel industries was a tax on fuel and heating oils (equivalent, when first imposed in 1961 at 0·83 pence per gallon, to over 30 per cent of the pre-tax price of heavy fuel oil). This tax protected coal from oil competition and fundamentally affected the energy market in numerous ways. Whether intentionally or not, it also gave some protection to nuclear power *vis-à-vis* oil in electricity generation and to natural gas which, by the late 1960s, was being produced from the British North Sea.

The confusion which surrounded energy policy in the early 1960s can be appreciated from the remark made by the then Chancellor of the Exchequer (Selwyn Lloyd) in introducing the fuel oil tax in his 1961 Budget that it was purely a means of raising revenue.[10] The Ministry of Power evidently knew nothing about the tax until it was announced. It may have been that no one considered its likely long-term consequences; alternatively, since political time-horizons are short, no one in government may have been concerned at what those consequences might be.

By the time the White Papers appeared, other 'fuel policy' measures in existence were the restrictions on coal imports mentioned above, a virtual ban on Soviet oil imports and preference for coal in the power generation and local authority markets. The nationalised coal industry's debts were written down in 1965 and assistance was provided for miners displaced by the contraction of the industry. Later, as North

---

10   Robinson, *A Policy for Fuel?, op. cit.,* pp.17-18.

Sea natural gas production began in 1968, governments let it be known that the Central Electricity Generating Board (CEGB) would not be permitted to burn more than token volumes of natural gas in its power stations. The *de facto* ban on gas sales for power generation was intended principally to protect coal in its main market.[11]

Nuclear Power – 'Too Cheap to Meter'?

Several important steps affecting civil nuclear power were also taken in the 1950s and 1960s.[12] Governments of both major parties promoted nuclear power programmes, supporting the technology with large sums of money, ostensibly because it was regarded as a means of filling the 'energy gap' which they foresaw and of diversifying fuel supplies to enhance security.

However, in the background another powerful group was hard at work, pressing the government to support its interests. In some ways it was as successful as the miners. The Atomic Energy Authority (AEA), formed in 1954, worked more subtly than the coal industry: it had an information monopoly and it relied on blinding governments with science. Its claim was that its wonderful new technology would before long produce power 'too cheap to meter' if only government would provide the necessary funds. As a consequence the government was persuaded that Britain should embark on a civil nuclear power programme based on British-designed Magnox reactors (which used carbon dioxide as a coolant and graphite as a moderator). The first nuclear power programme, announced in 1955, was aimed at building 12 stations with a total capacity of between 1,500 and 2,000MW by 1965. Within two years, following the 1956 Suez crisis and an upsurge of optimism about the prospects for nuclear power, the programme was approximately tripled in size to 5,000-6,000MW. Subsequently, following numerous technical

---

11 Robinson, *Zeitschrift für Energie Wirtschaft, op. cit.*, and 'Energy Trends and the Development of Energy Policy in the United Kingdom', *op. cit.*

12 Duncan Burn, *The Political Economy of Nuclear Energy*, Research Monograph 9, London: IEA, 1967.

problems, the CEGB became disillusioned with the performance of Magnox reactors: the programme was reduced in size to 5,000MW and extended in time to 1968.

Despite the problems with Magnox, a second nuclear power programme followed, after a 1965 appraisal which purported to demonstrate that the British designed Advanced Gas Cooled Reactor (AGR) was superior on technical and economic grounds to the US Boiling Water Reactors with which it was compared. The AGR was an AEA design which was essentially a more advanced version of Magnox, using enriched uranium and operating at higher temperatures. The target for the second programme, announced in 1965, was 8,000MW of AGR capacity by 1975; in 1978, two more AGRs with a combined capacity of about 2,500MW were added. However, the plans fell far behind schedule. Construction times were greatly in excess of those anticipated, operating problems arose and costs turned out to be much higher than originally predicted.[13] Only recently have the last reactors in the AGR programme been fully commissioned – about 15 years behind schedule.

By the late 1960s, it was plain that British energy 'policy', directed first at sheltering the nationalised coal industry and second at promoting nuclear power – in both cases heavily influenced by powerful producer interest groups which were adept at exploiting the electoral hopes and fears of politicians – had produced unfortunate and unintended side-effects. The protective régime provided an environment in which competition among the fuels was limited, energy prices were therefore unnecessarily high, and security of supply was diminished by over-reliance on home-produced coal.

Electricity and Protection

Politicians implemented protection principally through the nationalised electricity supply industry. Fuel choices in the industry were under government influence. Its managers could easily be cajoled into using more British coal than they would

---

13   Colin Robinson, *The Power of the State*, London: Adam Smith Institute, 1991.

freely have chosen and into accepting British-designed nuclear reactors. Indeed, they provided more general support for British industry, for example through a 'Buy British' policy for generating plant. Although this policy increased generating costs, the market power of the monopoly generator (the Central Electricity Generating Board) meant that any additional costs for which government did not provide direct compensation could be passed on to consumers. At times, such as the mid-1970s, when nationalised industry prices were held down by governments, the burden of protection shifted, at the margin, towards the taxpayer and away from the electricity consumer.

Taxation of oil, the fuel which had begun to pose a serious competitive threat to the coal and nuclear industries, blunted competition from the oil companies not only for coal and nuclear power but also for the emerging natural gas industry. But under the interventionist policies of the 1960s, even the oil companies were to an extent sheltered from competition by the exclusion of Soviet oil and overseas coal. Policy provided something for everyone, though there is no doubt that British coal was favoured above others.

The Late 1960s to the Mid-1980s: the North Sea, the World Oil 'Crisis' and the Coal Strike

For several years after publication of the 1967 White Paper, the trend towards increasing support for indigenously-produced fuels continued. The fuel oil tax was increased to 1 pence per gallon in 1968, the NCB's accumulated deficits were written off after miners' strikes in 1972 and 1973-74, the value of the Board's assets was written down again in 1973, and a Coal Industry Act in 1973 provided for £720 million in grants over the subsequent five years.[14]

However, Britain's fuel situation was changing towards what the 1967 White Paper described as a 'four fuel economy'. Nuclear power was the third fuel (after coal and oil); more

---

14 See note 11 above, p.21.

[23]

important, natural gas discoveries in the North Sea had provided a new source of indigenous energy supply from 1968 onwards which it was clear governments wished to exploit rapidly.[15]

The Significance of the North Sea

Even more significant were the oil discoveries in the northern North Sea from 1969 onwards. Discovery of the major British offshore fields in the first half of the 1970s coincided with a period of rapidly rising crude oil prices. It was a time of general concern about future energy shortages and unease about dependence on imported oil. Consequently, just as the internal energy situation was changing fundamentally, the international energy environment also became radically different.

Public awareness of energy matters was heightened from 1973 onwards as the news media concentrated on events in the oil market. Apparent shortages of gasoline, electricity and other fuels, particularly at the time of the first oil 'shock' in 1973-74, focussed attention on energy matters. The two principal producer interest groups – the coal industry and the nuclear power lobby – exploited the situation by arguing that indigenous producers should be supported by government in their efforts to replace imported fuels which, they claimed, were insecure and would inevitably increase further in price.

The 'Energy Issue'

As the 'energy issue' crossed the threshold of public awareness, the production of policies in the energy area appeared worthwhile to politicians anxious to capture votes. Governments in Britain and abroad had an incentive to appear busy producing policies which, whether they had any beneficial effect or not, would convince the electorate how assiduous they were in dealing with the problems which had

---

15 *North Sea Oil and Gas*, First Report from the Committee of Public Accounts, House of Commons, Session 1972-73, London: HMSO, 1973, para.96.

evidently emerged. The International Energy Agency was established in 1974, as a grouping of countries which were primarily consumers (rather than producers) of energy. At the same time, the so-called energy 'crisis' assumed such political importance that world leaders discussed it at a special 'summit' in Tokyo in June 1979.

Selective Taxation of Oil

In Britain, where North Sea discoveries and miners' strikes as well as the actions of OPEC received widespread media coverage, there was considerable government activity in the mid-1970s, much of it concerned with offshore oil.[16] An oil taxation régime was established by the Oil Taxation Act of 1975 which provided for selective taxation of oil-producing companies: as well as Corporation Tax, a royalty (a percentage tax on revenues common in most oil-producing areas) and a new tax on profits from production (Petroleum Revenue Tax) were applied.

There were numerous changes to a rather complex system over the next few years: the general effect was a very high marginal tax rate on profits from the fields developed in the 1970s of about 85 per cent and an average rate of some 70 per cent. Such high rates clearly diminished the incentive to hold down costs. They also reduced the sensitivity of production-related activities to price: the main effects of increases or decreases in crude oil prices were felt by the state, in terms of variations in tax receipts, rather than by the oil companies. Another effect of high taxes on oil production was that the bulk of the 'rent' from oil production was channelled to the state. On grounds of principle, it can be argued that one of the principal reasons why, in retrospect, it is so hard to see what benefits Britain derived from North Sea oil in the 1980s is that politicians were wasteful in their use of this large new source of tax revenues.

---

16 For an analysis of government policy in the early days of North Sea oil and gas, see Colin Robinson and Jon Morgan, *North Sea Oil in the Future*, London: Macmillan, 1978.

State 'Participation'

Given the climate of opinion, state 'participation' in the upstream oil industry became an issue in Britain in the 1970s. The British National Oil Corporation (BNOC), established by the Labour Government's 1975 Petroleum and Submarine Pipelines Act, was intended to bring a 'state presence' into the oil industry. It had certain privileges as compared with the private oil companies, such as exemption from Petroleum Revenue Tax and representation on oilfield operating committees; 51 per cent state participation gave it the right to purchase over half the oil produced in the North Sea.

Depletion Control

At about the same time, the Petroleum and Submarine Pipelines Act established a detailed mechanism for controlling the depletion rates of North Sea fields. In the mid-1970s, a prevailing view was that production cuts and development delays might be necessary in the 1980s when indigenous oil production seemed likely to be well in excess of indigenous oil consumption.[17] That was not just the view of the then Labour government: there was a consensus among the political parties that some means of regulating future production might be required, though they differed on the means of regulation.

In the event, no production cuts were made and the development of only one field (Clyde) was delayed: even that delay was probably not for depletion policy reasons but seems to have been motivated rather by a desire to keep down public sector borrowing (since Clyde was developed by BNOC).[18] The absence of any significant depletion control measures was partly because Conservative governments from 1979 onwards were, in principle, against interference with oil company activities. Probably more important, however, they were anxious to maximise tax revenues from oil production and to

---

17 *Ibid.*, p.30.

18 Colin Robinson, 'Oil Depletion Policy in the United Kingdom', *Three Banks Review*, September 1982, p.14.

obtain other macro-economic benefits. The tax yield rose sharply and became very large. In the peak year of North Sea tax revenues (1984-85), taxes on oil production amounted to about £12 billion – equivalent to some two-thirds of the yield from Value Added Tax in that year.[19]

Changing Coal Policy

Policy towards the British coal industry also changed after the 1973-74 oil price increases, although the changes were modifications of existing measures rather than new departures. The government endorsed the National Coal Board's 1974 *Plan for Coal* and its 1977 successor, *Coal for the Future*, which aimed at expanding the industry.[20] According to *Coal for the Future*, production of British coal could be expected by the year 2000 to have increased by about 37 per cent to 170 million tonnes. Coal subsidisation continued and the fuel oil tax was raised from 1 pence per gallon to 2·5p in 1977, 3p in 1979 and 3·5p in 1980.

The Conservative administration of 1979-83 at first seemed to want a progressive reduction in coal protection: those views were embodied in the 1980 Coal Industry Act which would have eliminated NCB deficit grants by 1983-84. However, after a threatened national miners' strike in February 1981, support for the coal industry was increased and coal imports for electricity generation were severely restricted.[21]

Even though Mrs Thatcher's first administration did little to change Britain's energy policy, there were signs that it had plans to do so. The Department of Energy became very reluctant to publish energy forecasts and plans, emphasising instead the desirability of promoting competition in the energy market. Indeed, in the International Energy Agency's 1982

---

19 Department of Trade and Industry, *Development of the Oil and Gas Resources of the United Kingdom* (annual), has details of the yields from North Sea taxation.

20 National Coal Board, *Plan for Coal*, 1974, and Department of Energy, *Coal for the Future*, 1977.

21 See Robinson and Marshall, *What Future for British Coal?*, *op. cit.*, Prologue.

review of British energy policy, its rapporteur commented on the government's unwillingness to produce 'most probable' supply and demand forecasts and to formulate '...a broad policy framework including a longer-term supply picture'.[22]

Precursors of Energy Privatisation

From 1982 onwards, several steps were taken which can now be seen as precursors of the energy privatisation programme which came in the Thatcher Government's third term. The British Gas Corporation's monopoly and monopsony powers were reduced under the Oil and Gas (Enterprise) Act of 1982 and its oil assets were sold as Enterprise Oil; BNOC's state trading arm was separated from its exploration and production activities which became Britoil and was later privatised; there were minor (and, as it turned out, ineffective) measures to facilitate private generation and distribution of electricity in the 1982 Energy Act; newspaper reports suggested that the electricity and gas industries might be candidates for privatisation;[23] and there seemed to be a threat to coal protection after publication of a critical Monopolies and Mergers Commission report.[24]

But the most important event which affected energy policy in the mid-1980s was the miners' strike from March 1984 to March 1985, early in the second term of the Thatcher Government. The result was generally perceived as a victory for the government. During the strike and subsequently, many pits were closed and many jobs were lost (as explained below). By the mid-1980s, the coal industry was far from the economic, political and social force it had been in the earlier post-war period. It could no longer put effective pressure on government, so the days of heavy protection for the industry

---

22 International Energy Agency, *Energy Policies and Programmes of IEA Countries*, 1982 Review, Paris: OECD, 1983, pp.361-79.

23 For example, 'Power supply review likely before sell-off', *The Financial Times*, 28 November 1983.

24 Monopolies and Mergers Commission, *National Coal Board*, Cmnd. 8920 (two volumes), London: HMSO, 1983.

seemed numbered. It is no coincidence that coal privatisation moved on to the political agenda around this time.[25]

Moreover, the nuclear industries were also becoming less effective lobbyists. Promises of cheap electricity from nuclear power had been continually falsified – not only in Britain but in most other countries – and construction delays, cost over-runs and technical problems in operation led politicians and civil servants to distrust views expressed by the industry. At the same time, two serious nuclear power station accidents, at Three Mile Island in the United States in 1979 and Chernobyl in the (then) Soviet Union in 1986, resulted in much-strengthened public opposition to the construction of new nuclear power plants and the continued operation of existing plants.

3. 1985 to the Present: Energy Privatisation

Privatisation – the Main Difference

IN TERMS OF POLICY towards the energy industries, the main difference between the period since 1985 and the earlier post-war years lies in the Thatcher administration's privatisation of the electricity and gas industries. Not only did those two industries move out of the state sector but the old protective policies towards indigenous energy suppliers were inevitably disturbed.

Privatisation was an important act of disengagement by government which was necessary if decisions in the energy industries were to become less politicised and if competition was to be allowed to develop. Nevertheless, privatisation – like nationalisation 40 years earlier – was a political act, heavily influenced by political considerations. As explained below, the privatisation schemes, especially for gas but also for electricity, introduced relatively little competition at the time of privatisation, relying instead on regulators and the competition authorities to liberalise markets over time.

---

25 Robinson, 'Coal Liberalisation: Retrospect and Prospect', *op. cit.*

There is room for differences of opinion on how much the initial structure of a privatised industry matters. It can be argued that, once privatisation has occurred in whatever form, the competitive process will work. Even a single incumbent with considerable market power will eventually find its position undermined because ingenious rivals will find ways of entering markets once there is no state protection of a monopoly position. Monopolies will in time disappear as the 'perennial gale of creative destruction' which Joseph Schumpeter emphasised sweeps through the economy.[26] Furthermore, potential rivals can be helped to establish themselves if regulators give them temporary assistance.

But establishing competitive markets from the beginning (where that is possible) brings benefits to consumers earlier rather than later and it may avoid adverse effects on industries associated with the privatised corporation(s) which may otherwise feel the effects of monopoly or monopsony power. Another important practical point is that, once governments have privatised in a particular form, they are reluctant to risk antagonising shareholders by acquiescing in schemes which regulators might recommend to break up the industries so as to speed the process of liberalisation.

Privatisation and Regulation

Privatisation schemes which introduce little competition initially also have consequences for regulation – in general they encourage it to be very wide-ranging. Indeed, it is a feature of all British utility privatisation schemes that failure to liberalise product markets under the terms of the original privatisations led to the application of regulation to naturally competitive parts of the industries. Lack of interest in market liberalisation – even from a government which professed to believe in competition – arises because privatisation is designed to meet political ends. Priority is given to achieving aims – such as raising substantial revenues and widening share

---

26 Joseph A. Schumpeter, *Capitalism, Socialism and Democracy*, London: Allen and Unwin, fifth edition, 1976, especially Chapter VII.

ownership – which are likely to provide a short-run return in terms of increased votes. Pursuing these aims, however, means making the privatised corporations attractive to potential shareholders which is most easily accomplished by leaving them with market power. Thus there is a conflict with market liberalising moves. Seen in that light, the very wide scope of regulation in privatised British utilities is a natural outcome of illiberal privatisation schemes.[27]

Some of the other consequences of gas and electricity privatisation are discussed below.

Gas Privatisation

Gas privatisation in 1986 was condemned by many economists because of its failure to liberalise the gas market. During its nationalised period British Gas had enjoyed a monopoly of gas distribution through pipes and virtual monopsony rights in the purchase of natural gas from producers in the North Sea. As a result the Corporation had a very strong entrenched position in gas supply and a powerful bargaining situation *vis-à-vis* North Sea gas producers. On privatisation, it would have been possible to have divided the corporation into a number of regional gas distributors and a national pipeline and storage company.[28] Such a division would have encouraged oil companies with gas production in the North Sea to have begun direct supply to larger consumers via an open access pipeline network or by constructing their own pipelines. Competition in gas supply would thus speedily have been established.

British Gas as a Pressure Group

However, at the time of privatisation British Gas showed that it was a powerful pressure group, able to match anything the

---

27 Colin Robinson, 'Public Choice Issues in UK Regulation', paper to Adam Smith Institute Conference on 'Regulating the Regulators', March 1993 (in Eamonn Butler (ed.), *But Who Will Regulate the Regulators?*, London: ASI, November 1993).

28 House of Commons Energy Committee, *Regulation of the Gas Industry*, Session 1985-86, London: HMSO, 1986, Memoranda 13 and 14.

coal and nuclear lobbies had been able to accomplish in earlier times, by securing a form of privatisation which maximised short-run benefits to management. It was privatised in essentially the same form as its nationalised predecessor, so its senior managers retained virtually all the market power they had previously enjoyed and at the same time had the greatly increased salaries and other benefits which accrue on transfer to the private sector. Although entry to gas supply was now possible, instead of being prohibited by the state, anyone wishing to enter gas supply in Great Britain faced an extremely strong and long-established incumbent supplier which controlled the pipeline network, and to which nearly all available North Sea gas was already contracted. So a significant interval seemed likely before the competitive process became effective. One of the consequences of emerging from privatisation with such obvious market power was that, as impatience mounted with the slow pace at which competition in gas supply materialised, so British Gas eventually brought on itself the full force of a regulatory régime which tried to act as a countervailing force by promoting competition.[29]

The First MMC Reference...

Within a year of privatisation, after complaints that the British Gas Corporation (BGC) was abusing its monopoly position in the industrial market, it was referred to the Monopolies and Mergers Commission (MMC). The MMC's report in October 1988,[30] though not proposing structural changes, made a number of recommendations intended to stimulate some competition in the gas market. The three most important were:

o BGC should not be permitted to contract to purchase more than 90 per cent of the output of new North Sea gas fields.

29 Colin Robinson, 'Privatising the British Energy Industries: the lessons to be learned', *Metroeconomica*, Vol.XLIII, No.1-2, February-June 1992.

30 Monopolies and Mergers Commission, *Gas*, Cm. 500, London: HMSO, 1988.

o It should publish a schedule of gas tariffs to contract customers.

o It should publish the rates at which it would be willing to transport gas for other suppliers through its pipeline system.

The MMC's objectives were to reduce BGC's monopsony power, freeing some North Sea gas for suppliers other than British Gas; to allow entrants and potential entrants which wished to supply gas to large consumers to see what rates were being charged by BGC; and to provide access for those entrants to BGC's extensive pipeline network.

...and Action by OFGAS

The Office of Gas Regulation (Ofgas), headed by Mr (now Sir) James McKinnon, which has the duty to promote competition, was from the beginning insistent that British Gas should ease entry into gas supply. After a number of battles with the company, it proposed in 1990 that BGC relinquish its rights to some gas supplies for which it had already contracted in order to speed up the introduction of competition: the aim was that 30 per cent of the firm contract gas market (excluding sales to power generation) should be supplied by BGC's competitors by 1993.[31] After some resistance, BGC offered to surrender to competitors 150 million cubic feet a day of gas (equivalent to about 10 per cent of the industrial gas market). The gas would be available until October 1992 and would have to be repaid over the next five years.[32] The power generation market for gas, which grew rapidly in the early 1990s as the government lifted the ban on gas sales for electricity generation, was competitive from the beginning: it was relatively easy for North Sea producers to

---

[31] 'Regulating the Future for Gas Suppliers', speech by James McKinnon to NEMEX 1990, London, 4 December 1990.

[32] 'British Gas may cede 10 per cent of market', *The Financial Times*, 31 January 1991.

supply power stations direct and so they quickly gained a bigger market share than BGC.

The OFT Joins In

More radical proposals to enhance competition were contained in a 1991 report by the Office of Fair Trading. The main proposals were that BGC should separate its pipeline and storage system from the rest of its operations, either by sale or at least by placing it in a separate subsidiary; that some of its contracted gas supplies should be sold to competitors; that gas imports should be freed; and that the prohibition on supply by competitors to consumers of less than 25,000 therms a years should be eased, with a new threshold of 2,500 therms a year and possibly no limits at all from 1996 onwards.[33] The government accepted the proposed lowering of the threshold to 2,500 therms from 1993 onwards with the idea of bringing many consumers (including larger residential users) within the competitive market.

Intrusive Regulation

By the latter part of 1992, however, BGC was becoming increasingly concerned at what it saw as the intrusiveness of gas industry regulation. Intrusiveness was inevitable, given the amount of market power BGC had possessed on privatisation and given the regulator's duty to promote competition. Had the government at the time of privatisation placed the pipeline and storage system in a separate company and taken other measures to liberalise the gas market, regulation could have been confined to the natural monopoly sector of the gas industry (the network of pipelines). Consumers would have been protected by competition, and possibly by temporary price regulation for domestic consumers until competition developed in that market. But, as it was, BGC's concern about the intrusiveness of gas regulation was such that, whilst

---

33 'Lilley pledges more gas competition', *The Financial Times*, 11 October 1991, and 'British Gas feels the heat of competition policy', *The Financial Times*, 17 October 1991.

negotiations were in progress about the rate of return appropriate to the BGC pipeline network under threat of another MMC reference, the company itself decided to refer the whole gas business to the MMC.[34]

The Second MMC Report

The second MMC report[35] appeared in August 1993 and was much more radical than the first, making recommendations which, if accepted by the government, will significantly enhance competition in the British gas market. One important recommendation was that British Gas should divest itself of its trading activities by 1997 (with accounting separation of those activities within BGC in 1994) so that it will become an exploration, production, pipeline and storage company in Britain but no longer a trader in gas. Implementing that recommendation would help to remove the conflict of interest, inherent in the privatisation scheme, of ownership by British Gas (hitherto the main gas trader) of the pipeline and storage system which potential competitors must use. Entry to the gas supply business would be considerably easier as a consequence.

Under another MMC recommendation, competition would be extended to smaller consumers than at present because the British Gas monopoly would from 1997 be confined to consumers of less than 1,500 therms a year with the intention of abolishing the monopoly by early next century.

Electricity Privatisation

The Scheme

Under the electricity privatisation plan for England and Wales, set out in a White Paper of February 1988,[36] the Central Electricity Generating Board was divided into a

---

34 'Simmering row comes into the open', *The Financial Times*, 3 August 1992.

35 Monopolies and Mergers Commission, *Gas and British Gas plc*, Cm.2316, London: HMSO, 1993.

36 *Privatising Electricity*, Cm.322, London: HMSO, 1988.

transmission company (the National Grid Company) and two large generators (National Power and PowerGen). Twelve Regional Electricity Companies (RECs), based on their predecessor Area Boards, were established to distribute and supply electricity, though supply to larger consumers is subject to competition among the RECs and from the generators. By 1998, there will in principle be competition among generators and RECs to supply all consumers. In practice, smaller consumers are likely for some years to be supplied by their local RECs and they will be protected from exploitation of local monopoly power by the Office of Electricity Regulation (OFFER). Regulatory price control is based on the RPI-X+Y mechanism common to the privatised utilities in Britain.[37]

RECs are also permitted to generate a small proportion of the electricity they supply though it is not intended that there should be any substantial degree of vertical integration except in Scotland where changes in industry structure are more limited, as compared with nationalisation, than in England and Wales. Scotland still has two vertically integrated power companies (Scottish Power and Scottish Hydro).

A Better Structure than Gas?

Compared with the illiberal gas privatisation scheme, electricity privatisation was better directed at introducing competition to the electricity market. For instance, there is a separate transmission organisation, open access to both the transmission network and local distribution systems at specified use-of-system charges, and a splitting of the CEGB rather than privatisation intact as in the case of British Gas. Nevertheless, as in other privatisations, the management of the nationalised industry produced a stream of reasons (many relating to the technical characteristics of the industry) why the market should not be liberalised. Those views, though to

---

37 The aim of the formula is to allow prices of the regulated company to increase by the amount of the increase in the retail price index (RPI) but with a deduction (X) to give it an incentive to improve efficiency and, in some cases, an addition (Y) for costs which are believed to be outside the company's control.

some extent discounted, had an influence on the privatisation scheme and were one of the reasons why the government adopted an unsatisfactory duopolistic structure of generation in England and Wales.

Another reason for the establishment of the duopoly is that the government originally intended to privatise nuclear power and wanted to establish a large generator in which existing nuclear stations (many of which were, at the time, performing poorly) would not be too obtrusive. The idea was to embed existing nuclear plant in National Power (the larger generator) which was also to be given responsibility for the new programme of nuclear construction of four Pressurised Water Reactors (PWRs) which was then planned.

The Failed Attempt to Privatise Nuclear Power

However, the attempt to privatise nuclear power failed. It was received very badly by potential investors who were reluctant to invest in a company exposed to the kinds of unforeseeable risks they perceived to follow from operating existing nuclear plant, constructing new stations and decommissioning plants at the end of their lives.[38] In effect, the capital markets vetoed the attempt to privatise nuclear power stations. Consequently, in July 1989, the government decided to keep the existing ageing Magnox stations in the public sector; a similar decision about the AGRs was made in November 1989. Two new state-owned companies were established - Nuclear Electric for the English and Welsh nuclear stations and Scottish Nuclear for the stations in Scotland. Only one PWR (Sizewell 'B') is under construction (due for completion in 1994). The proposal to build three more PWRs was dropped though it could still be revived: a government review of nuclear power prospects, due in 1994, may begin before the end of 1993.

Novel Features of the Industry

Some novel features of the new structure of the electricity supply industry in Britain are likely eventually to lead to more

---

38 Robinson, *The Power of the State, op. cit.*

competition in the generation and supply of electricity than exists in most other countries. Though it is difficult to enter electricity generation because of the power of the incumbent generators, nevertheless since entry used to be impossible the new régime is an improvement on the old. Technological change – especially the availability of combined cycle gas turbine plant, which is relatively low-cost and can be constructed in about three years (compared with nearer 10 years for coal plant under the CEGB) – has helped to ease entry by reducing the minimum efficient scale of operation.[39]

Lowering Entry Barriers

As barriers to entering electricity generation are lowered, prospective entrants are likely to form expectations that they can come into the market and make profits. If that is so, incumbents will face actual and potential rivals. Thus, the initial market power of those incumbents will in the end be much diminished. Not only should competition in generation appear, but competition in supply should follow as new generators use their access to the transmission and distribution networks to supply larger consumers.

Some competition in supply has appeared (among National Power, PowerGen, new entrants to generation in England and Wales, the Scottish companies, the nuclear companies, the RECs and imports from France), though its effect on prices is confused by the disappearance of special price arrangements which, under nationalisation, applied to electricity supplied to very large consumers.

Moreover, there are a number of questions which must be resolved before a rivalrous electricity generation market can be anticipated in the foreseeable future. Much of the entry into

---

39 Colin Robinson and Allen Sykes, 'Privatising Electricity Supply', Memorandum 48 in *The Structure, Regulation and Economic Consequences of Electricity Supply in the Private Sector*, Third Report of the House of Commons Energy Committee, Session 1987-88, HC307-II, London: HMSO, 1988, and Colin Robinson, Memorandum, in *Consequences of Electricity Privatisation*, Report of the House of Commons Energy Committee, Session 1991-92, HC 113-III, London: HMSO, 1992.

generation so far is by companies which are related, either by equity stake (in most cases fairly small) or by long-term contract, to incumbents. Independent entry is required if competition is to flourish in the industry.

Another issue is that the two large generators are perceived (rightly or wrongly) to be using their market power to restrict competition and to manipulate prices in the electricity pooling system for England and Wales. The influence of newcomers on pool prices is limited because their plant runs almost continually on base load; the major generators have the marginal power stations which set prices under the pooling system.

Uncertainty about pool prices may be a deterrent to entry into the market; it may be one of the reasons that entrants seem willing to come into the British market only in association with incumbent electricity companies, though it is perhaps not surprising that entrants to a new kind of market seek and obtain long-term contracts.

The Wide Scope of Regulation

Although electricity privatisation (unlike gas) introduced a measure of competition from the beginning, OFFER, like OFGAS, has – because of the limitations of the privatisation scheme – inevitably been drawn into regulating parts of the industry which cannot be regarded as 'natural monopolies'.

In the case of electricity, the scope of regulation clearly goes well beyond any reasonable definition of the naturally monopolistic parts of the industry. The network of wires existing at the time of privatisation, both in the National Grid Company network and in the distribution systems of the RECs is, with existing technology, naturally monopolistic (though there is no good reason to grant NGC and the RECs exclusive rights to add to the network). In the rest of the industry competition is both necessary and desirable. But it is constrained by the nature of the privatisation scheme and, in particular, by the market power of the two major generators.

OFFER has therefore necessarily been drawn into regulating the generators: on several occasions, it has investigated the activities of National Power and PowerGen in bidding into the pool.[40] If one regards regulation as an unsatisfactory last resort which is incapable of simulating the results of competitive markets (see Section 5 below), the very wide scope of regulation in electricity is a matter for considerable concern. Not only is OFFER having to regulate a part of the industry in which the benefits of competition could have been realised, but it is also being diverted from the task of regulating those sectors which (given present technology) are naturally monopolistic.

Electricity Privatisation, Energy Policy and the Coal Industry

The significance of electricity privatisation goes beyond the British government's decision to return to the private sector a particularly complex industry. Important also are the implications for energy policy and, as a consequence, for the British energy market as a whole.

As explained above, the electricity supply industry was for many years the focus for most of the protective measures in the British fuel market. It was inconceivable that it could be moved from the public to the private sector without undermining that protective structure. Support for coal, already threatened by the 'defeat' of the National Union of Mineworkers in the 1984-85 strike, was bound to be questioned as fuel choice decisions in electricity supply (coal's biggest customer) came to be made by private companies rather than by nationalised corporations subject to strong political influence. For similar reasons, the policy of promoting nuclear power was also endangered by the privatisation of electricity.

Fundamental Changes in Energy Policy

Electricity privatisation did indeed turn out to be the occasion for fundamental changes in government policy towards the

---

40 Office of Electricity Regulation: *Report on Pool Price Inquiry*, December 1991; *Report on Gas Turbine Plant*, June 1992; *Report on Constrained-on Plant*, October 1992; *Pool Price Statement*, July 1993, Birmingham: OFFER.

energy industries, though it coincided with, or followed soon after a number of other events all of which pointed in the direction of a less protectionist régime in energy. The most significant of those events were the coal strike (1984-85) and its outcome, gas privatisation (1986) and its aftermath, the ending at the time of electricity privatisation of the government ban on gas sales for power generation, the EC's environmental regulations of 1988 which restrict emissions of sulphur,[41] and a more hostile attitude to nuclear power in Britain after revelations about its costs during the electricity privatisation debates.[42]

But the policy of supporting coal, which had persisted throughout the post-war period, was the most obvious casualty of electricity privatisation. The coal and electricity supply industries were closely linked, not least by government-inspired contracts which, from 1979 onwards, protected coal by inducing the electricity supply industry to burn more British coal than it would freely have taken.[43] Because of these contracts the nationalised coal industry, which had enjoyed well-diversified sales as recently as the late 1950s, concentrated nearly all its efforts on selling into electricity generation (Figure 2): in the early 1990s over 80 per cent of British Coal sales were to that market. It was therefore dangerously exposed to any change in the market for generation fuels.

The Limited Early Impact on Coal

In the early stages of privatised electricity, the impact on the British coal industry was limited because the government insisted that, over the three years to March 1993, the two major generators should contract with British Coal for much more coal (70 million tonnes a year, falling to 65 million

---

41 House of Commons Energy Committee, *The Flue Gas Desulphurisation Programme*, Third Report, Session 1989-90, HC 371, London: HMSO, 1990.

42 Robinson, *The Power of the State, op. cit.*

43 Robinson and Marshall, *Can Coal Be Saved?, op. cit.*, p.35.

[41]

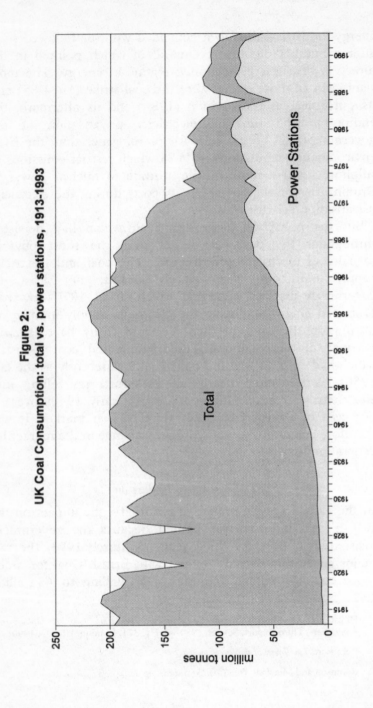

Figure 2:
UK Coal Consumption: total vs. power stations, 1913-1993

tonnes a year) than they would freely have used. From April 1993, the contract volumes were much smaller (40 million tonnes falling to 30 million tonnes a year) but that was not all. There was a huge overhang of stocks because the quantities under the initial contracts had been far larger than the generators' consumption of coal. Just before the initial contracts expired, British Coal therefore proposed a very big contraction in the industry (see below, p.44) to bring output into line with likely demand.

The imminent end of coal protection is a welcome development. As explained above, the policy was very bad for British energy consumers. Moreover, it was bad for British coal, as protection almost always is for sheltered industries which inevitably fail to show the entrepreneurship and innovative ability of firms which operate in competitive conditions. Nevertheless, just as the policy was inappropriate so the way in which it is being ended leaves a great deal to be desired.

A Lost Opportunity

In the 1980s the government had an opportunity, which it failed to take, to privatise coal. Although it was announced at the 1988 Conservative Party conference as 'the ultimate privatisation',[44] nothing was done to proceed with coal privatisation. Instead the government privatised electricity, establishing two major generators which, given coal's dependence on electricity generation, clearly had substantial bargaining power relative to British Coal. There was no indication of the structure of privatised coal nor of when privatisation might occur. In an industry already in decline, the effect on morale of this state of extreme uncertainty was devastating. The industry's attractiveness both to existing staff and to potential recruits was greatly diminished and a redundancy culture emerged: miners seemed only too anxious

---

44 'Parkinson looks to coal as "ultimate privatisation" ', *The Financial Times*, 13 October 1988.

for their pits to close so that they could take the generous redundancy terms on offer before it was too late. It is hardly surprising that the industry contracted rapidly. Figure 3, which shows numbers employed in coal-mining since the beginning of the century, places the recent decline in perspective.

The Scale of Contraction

On the eve of the 1984-85 strike there were about 180,000 miners working in 170 pits, but by October 1992 there were only 40,000 in 51 pits. British Coal then announced a plan to close another 31 pits and to reduce its workforce by another 30,000 (including white collar workers as well as miners).[45] The government called a moratorium on pit closures and then spent some months reviewing British Coal's proposed closure programme, publishing the results in its 'Coal and Energy Review' of March 1993,[46] temporarily raising hopes that not all the 31 would close. But by the Autumn of 1993 it seemed likely that most (if not all) of the planned closures would go ahead: indeed, there might be more closures than proposed in October 1992.

Productivity increased very sharply from the late 1980s onwards: output per manshift worked rose at an annual average compound rate of over 15 per cent from 1988 to mid-1993. Nevertheless, the increase was insufficient to price British coal back into an electricity market which had massive stocks (because of the excessive purchases of coal the generators had been forced to make in the first three years of privatisation), in which nuclear power was still subsidised, and where large amounts of gas-fired plant were under construction or already commissioned.

---

45 Colin Robinson, *Making a Market in Energy*, Current Controversies No.3, London: IEA, December 1992.

46 Department of Trade and Industry, *The Prospects for Coal: Conclusions of the Government's Coal Review*, Cm.2235, London: HMSO, 1993.

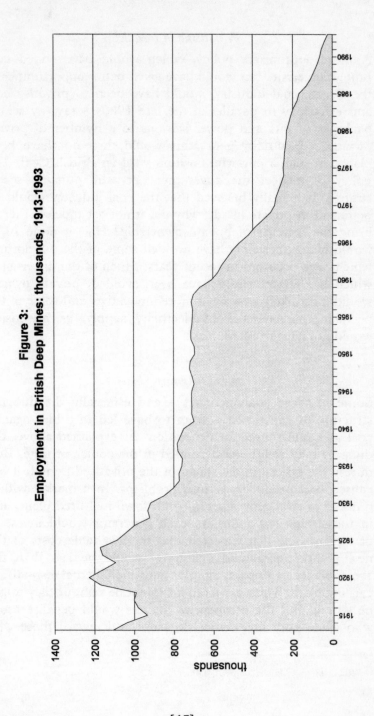

Figure 3:
Employment in British Deep Mines: thousands, 1913-1993

A more appropriate policy, which would have ended coal protection earlier but would have given better opportunities to the British coal industry, would have been to privatise coal and electricity in parallel in the late 1980s – say, by selling packages of pits and power stations to a number of private owners.[47] Electricity generators would then not have been placed in such a powerful position *vis-à-vis* British Coal. The policy of neglect the government actually pursued seems strange. If it really believed that the coal industry would be better off in private hands, why did it not act much earlier to bring the benefits of private ownership? Had it done so, it would almost certainly have avoided some of the pit closures which have occurred in recent years. Much of the uncertainty which has arisen would have been avoided, private owners would most likely have been more innovative, and some of the peculiar characteristics of electricity supply, as privatised, would not have resulted.

A Bias Against Coal?

Some of these characteristics – and especially the duopoly structure of generation – seem to have led to a bias against coal as a fuel source for generation. As explained above, the duopoly may well be undermined in the course of time. But, during the crucial initial stages of the privatised period, it has caused coal producers serious problems. In a market with a number of rival generators, all with fossil fuel-fired plant, and in the absence of collusion, each generator would invest in new plant only if it expected that the avoidable costs of the new plant (capital and operating) would be less than the avoidable costs (operating plus any incremental capital) of existing plant. Their expectations might be right or they might be wrong. But the competitive process would penalise those who made poor fuel choice decisions and reward those who

---

47   Robinson and Marshall, *op. cit.*, p.45.

made better decisions. It would therefore provide incentives to make better fuel choices than one's competitors.

However, in a market where all coal-fired plant has been divided between two companies, each of which is a successor of the CEGB and each of which therefore is likely to have reasonable knowledge of the other's costs, the competitive process is unlikely to work so well. Fuel choices will probably not be the same as those which would have been made in a market with more rival producers. The duopolists have sufficient market power (given them by government) to indulge in strategic gaming so as to maintain their own positions at the expense of potential newcomers.

Exactly how that power will be exercised is necessarily somewhat uncertain. But some bias against the use of existing coal-fired plant seems a likely result. The major generators may well, for example, have some incentive to announce plans to build new gas plant as a means of pre-empting entry to generation: they know that entry will only be with gas-fired stations since they are perceived to be lower cost than other new plant. Even if their own estimates suggest that it would have been cheaper to keep existing coal stations in operation, they may announce such plans as a means of entry deterrence: because of their market power, they are unlikely to be constrained from passing on to the RECs and large consumers the costs of the choices they make. Moreover, because the two major generators, between them, control the bulk of generating capacity in England and Wales, they can accelerate their plant closure programmes if capacity shows signs of becoming excessive.[48]

Another problem which arises from the duopoly and which favours the construction of new gas stations is that the RECs have an incentive to avoid the market power of the generators. Thus they will tend to build more new plant themselves (or sign long-term contracts with owners of new plant) than they would have done had generation been competitive. Most of

---

48 Robinson, *Making a Market in Energy*, op. cit.

the RECs have little existing generation and so they do not consider the alternative of keeping open coal- or oil-fired power stations.

4. Conclusions on Post-War Energy Policy

WHAT CONCLUSIONS can be drawn from this brief survey of British energy policy over a period of nearly 50 years? It is a story, in essence familiar from other examples, of the powerful influence which producer pressure groups exert on policy; governments have little incentive to pay regard to the interests of consumers who are generally unorganised and appear unable to deliver votes on the same scale as the producers. So, as actual or supposed problems arise, organised groups press government to take actions which will serve their interests – and they have considerable success.

Benefits to Producers, Not Consumers

Government actions are therefore directed not towards serving the welfare of consumers, as supporters of 'energy policies' seem generally to suppose, but to the interests of producers. 'Policies' are not wise, long-term strategies, conceived after disinterested analysis of the options, but the products of short-termism, aimed at gaining political advantage.

Politicians are susceptible to arguments that large numbers of jobs (and, by implication, votes) might be lost because of the decline of a particular fuel industry and to claims from suppliers with complex technologies that they are capable, given a few years of taxpayer support, of producing large quantities of cheap energy. Hence British Coal and the NUM were for many years successful in maintaining extensive protection for the nationalised coal industry and the nuclear lobby obtained huge sums from government to satisfy its desire for a programme of British-designed reactors. Eventual effects on consumers of pursuing protectionist policies receive little attention. The effects take many years to appear, by which time a different administration may be in power. In any case, it is difficult to trace back such effects to the originating government actions.

Producers and Privatisation

When privatisation schemes are being considered, lobbying from producer groups is also a very important factor.[49] Politicians are not particularly interested in liberalising markets via privatisation: the effects show up only in the medium- to long-term and cannot easily be identified with the privatisation scheme, so the opportunities for capturing votes are limited. Governments are inclined to favour less liberal schemes, influenced by the managements of the nationalised corporations (which are in a position to hinder plans which they do not favour), which leave substantial market power in the hands of the privatised companies. In general, these less liberal schemes are appealing to potential shareholders (since, other things equal, companies with more market power will appear likely to be more profitable): thus more revenues will be raised for government and there will be more shareholder-voters appreciative of having received shares at a substantial discount. Hence, British Gas management found it not too difficult to persuade government that the company should be privatised intact, and the CEGB and other parts of the nationalised electricity supply industry were able, with some success, to deploy the argument that the lights might go out if there were more than a token split of generation.

The recent history of government action in British energy markets provides ample evidence that it has been short-termist, producer-driven and subject to sudden and sharp change. However, that is merely a description of the past. Despite such an unhappy history, one cannot conclude without further evidence that policy must necessarily perform so badly. Perhaps energy policies *could* be conceived and executed for the benefit of the community as a whole rather than mainly for producers. In other words, the problems described above may not be inherent in energy policies: wise

---

49   Robinson, *Metroeconomica, op. cit.*

and enlightened people, acting in the general interest, might be able to do better. What substance is there in such arguments?

5. The Case for an Energy Policy

DESPITE PAST EXPERIENCE, most proponents of energy policy seem to think it so obviously desirable as not to require explicit defence or even definition. They take refuge in generalities such as the supposed 'strategic' characteristics of energy or the supposed responsibility of government for the security of energy supply or, more recently, the necessity for government to take into account the environmental effects associated with energy production, transportation and consumption.

Occasionally, the case appears in more respectable form, discussing a number of externalities which markets are supposed to fail to take into account. However, believers in energy policy mostly seem unaware of how real-world governments behave and they commit the sin of comparing the results of imperfect markets with the results they infer from the actions of perfect governments: the behaviour of a perfect government cannot, of course, be observed since there is no such thing, any more than there is a perfect market.

It is best to consider the case for an energy policy by examining first the general advantages of permitting markets to work and the disadvantages of government action. Then we can consider the extent to which markets might fail.

The Case for Markets

The case for leaving energy affairs mainly to markets has two strands. One is positive – that markets have such desirable characteristics that they have no close substitutes. The other is negative – the alternative of government action is so undesirable that it should be avoided wherever feasible.

To begin with the negative case, public choice theorists and Chicago-school empirical researchers have so clearly demonstrated the serious problems inherent in government action that the traditional *deus ex machina* case which used to be made by old-style welfare economists (that government could always be brought in to set to rights the mess markets were making) is surely untenable. That, however, does not prevent the old-fashioned case from being put forward by politicians, civil servants, Parliamentary committees, journalists and even some economists.

The Problems of Government Action

To summarise, the principal problems of government action are:[50]

o *First,* elections are an exchange of policies for votes but the market outcome is flawed because voters have little incentive to discover in detail what political parties will do when in office since the costs of finding such information are extremely high relative to the infinitesimal influence any individual has on the outcome of an election. It is, therefore, rational for voters to remain ignorant. The rationality of voter ignorance leads to sloganising, similar to that in advertising campaigns in oligopolistic (and particularly duopolistic) industries.

o *Second,* in representative political systems, governments, once in office, are the sole suppliers of policy: thus they have monopoly power and so the familiar problems of monopoly arise.

o *Third,* monopoly power in this case is particularly serious because governments can use that power to gain access to a very deep purse which consists of other people's money;

50 See, for example, Anthony Downs, *An Economic Theory of Democracy*, New York: Harper, 1957; Gordon Tullock, *The Vote Motive*, Hobart Paperback No.9, London: IEA, 1976; James M. Buchanan *et al.*, *The Economics of Politics*, IEA Readings No.18, IEA, 1978; W.C.Mitchell, *Government As It Is*, Hobart Paper No.109, IEA, 1988; and Arthur Seldon, 'Politicians for or against the people', in Gerard Radnitzky and Hardy Bouillon, *Government: Servant or Master?*, Amsterdam-Atlanta: Rodopi, 1993.

thus they are able to coerce citizens into financing their schemes.

o *Fourth*, governments are heavily influenced by producer pressure groups which appear able to deliver substantial numbers of votes; those groups respond rationally to politicised markets by lobbying – since any favours the government grants them will bring benefits to their members but will be paid for by others.

Government Failure

For such reasons, government failure is a serious problem. Indeed, it is so serious that, as Arthur Seldon has persuasively argued, there is something to be said for taking a risk on under-government.[51] The political market-place tends to lead to short-term decisions, taken in the hope of securing votes, on the basis of very poor quality information about the preferences of voters – because of the rationality of voter ignorance and because such information as does reach politicians is filtered by producer pressure groups which rush into the information vacuum (as we have seen they did in the British energy market in the post-war years). Moreover, because the system relies on majority voting it cannot provide for minorities in the ways that markets will do. The overall result is that, except by chance, the pursuit of political and bureaucratic self-interest will not be beneficial to the community (in contrast to the pursuit of self-interest in a competitive market).

The Reverse Invisible Hand

Of course, one does not have to assume that politicians and bureaucrats are malevolent to obtain this result, any more than one has to assume benevolence for the invisible hand to produce a socially desirable outcome from decisions which serve the self-interest of the decision-takers. Public choice

---

51 Seldon, *ibid.*, pp.3-21.

theorists would simply claim that people in the public sector are much the same as people in the private sector. But they have substantial monopoly power through which they can coerce and tax. They are not omniscient: they cannot define or discern the 'public interest' in any given case. Nor are they altruistic: they have their own interests to pursue. Consequently, as Milton Friedman has put it, there is a 'reverse invisible hand':

> 'People who intend to serve only the public interest are led by an invisible hand to serve private interests which was no part of their intention.'[52]

In this light, government is not the solution: it is the problem. It is quite extraordinary, given all the evidence about the way real-world governments behave, that so many people continue to recommend large-scale government action. Keynes would have seen the reason. It can be explained only by the continuing tendency of practical men to be the slaves of defunct economists.[53]

Markets and Discovery

The positive case for using markets rests primarily on the characteristics of markets as discovery processes. Whether or not markets are 'perfect' is irrelevant – there is nothing genuinely perfect or even particularly desirable about the perfect markets of economics textbooks. As Kirzner has said:

> 'What keeps the market process in motion is competition – *not* competition in the sense of "perfect competition", in which perfect knowledge is combined with very large numbers of buyers and sellers to generate a state of perennial equilibrium – but competition as the rivalrous activities of market participants trying

---

52 Milton Friedman, *Why Government is the Problem*, Stanford, CA: Hoover Institution, 1993, p.11.

53 'Practical men, who believe themselves to be quite exempt from any intellectual influences, are usually the slaves of some defunct economist.' (J.M.Keynes, *The General Theory of Employment, Interest and Money*, reprinted in *The Collected Writings of John Maynard Keynes*, Vol.VII, London: The Macmillan Press for the Royal Economic Society, 1973, p.383 (First Edn., Macmillan, 1936).)

to win profits by offering the market better opportunities than are currently available. The existence of rivalrous competition requires *not* large numbers of buyers and sellers but simply *freedom of entry* ... The competitive market process occurs because equilibrium has not yet been attained.'[54]

To see the fundamental reasons why markets work beneficially, one has to take an 'Austrian' perspective like Kirzner's which, following Hayek, sees knowledge as essentially dispersed: by definition, it cannot be gathered together in the hands of a few clever people in Whitehall or elsewhere.

The Impossibility of Accurate Forecasting

An awkward problem which faces each person is that he or she must make decisions which, by definition, are about the future. Yet all experience teaches us that we cannot know the future. We are all ignorant: *we do not even know what we do not know*. This dilemma is, strictly speaking, insoluble: each person must make forecasts, explicit or implicit, in order to run his or her life, yet forecasting is impossible. A competitive market, however, helps to solve this awkward problem because it is a mechanism for producing information which otherwise would not be known. In Kirzner's words:

'The competitive market process is needed not only to mobilise existing knowledge, but also to generate awareness of opportunities whose very existence until now has been known to no-one at all.'[55]

Effects of the Market Process

As entrepreneurs seek new ways of doing things, as consumers seek new products, discoveries will be made which would not

---

54 'The Perils of Regulation: A Market Process Approach', in Israel M.Kirzner, *Discovery and the Capitalist Process*, Chicago: University of Chicago Press, 1985, p.130.

55 *Ibid.*, p.131.

Energy Policy:
Errors, Illusions and Market Realities
COLIN ROBINSON

1. Britain has never had an energy policy, though governments have intervened in haphazard fashion in the energy market.

2. Post-war policies towards the energy industries were heavily influenced by two powerful interest groups – the coal and nuclear industries – which were the principal beneficiaries of 'energy policy'.

3. In energy privatisation schemes, politicians and producer groups had a common interest in restricting competition. In both gas and electricity, little competition was introduced initially. Liberalisation is occurring through the efforts of regulators and the Monopolies and Mergers Commission.

4. Although it was right to end coal protection, the structure of privatised electricity and the long period of uncertainty to which coal has been subjected have devastated British coalmining.

5. The Government missed an opportunity to privatise coal and electricity in parallel in the 1980s.

6. Recent history shows that 'energy policy' has been 'short-termist, producer-driven and subject to sudden and sharp change'.

7. There is a strong case for letting market forces work in energy, partly because of government failure but also because rivalrous (not 'perfect') competition will lead to a beneficial discovery process.

8. The discovery process will stimulate entrepreneurship and innovation, enhance security of supply and reduce costs and prices. It cannot be reproduced by government control or regulation.

9. Most arguments for a specific policy towards energy (for example, that it will increase security, improve the balance of payments, protect against rising fuel prices, safeguard future generations and protect the environment) have little substance.

10. A policy for energy is not only unnecessary but undesirable. It hampers market adjustment and induces producers to spend time influencing government rather than improving efficiency.

ISBN 0-255 36326-5 IEA Occasional Paper 90

The Institute of Economic Affairs
2 Lord North Street, Westminster
London SW1P 3LB
Telephone: 071-799 3745

£5.50 inc. p.+p.

IEA PUBLICATIONS
SUBSCRIPTION SERVICE

An annual subscription is the most convenient way to obtain our publications. Every title we produce in all our regular series will be sent to you immediately on publication and without further charge, representing a substantial saving.

Individual subscription rates* for 1993

Britain:	£30·00 p.a.
	£28·00 p.a. if paid by Banker's Order.
	£18·00 p.a. to teachers and students who pay *personally*.
Europe:	£30·00 p.a.
Rest of the world:	£40·00 p.a. Surface Mail; Airmail Rates on application.

* These rates are *not* available to companies or to institutions.

To: The Treasurer,
     Institute of Economic Affairs,
     2 Lord North Street,
     Westminster,
     LONDON SW1P 3LB

I should like to subscribe from: Month:.................................

Year:.....................

[Subscription can be taken out for past years; please indicate which you would like to include.]

☐ I enclose a cheque made payable to

The Institute of Economic Affairs for £............................

☐ Please charge my Access / Barclaycard / Diners Club / American Express / Visa / Mastercard

Number.............................. Expiry Date...................

NAME AND ADDRESS (Please print)

....

....

....

.... Postcode....................

Signature................................. Date.........................

I am a teacher/student at ....

.... (where applicable)

OP90

otherwise have been made. The forecasts on which people base decisions are imperfect but competitive forecasting and decision-making, and the discovery process which comes into operation as decisions are made, generate new knowledge.

Moreover, the market will also co-ordinate actions which otherwise could not have been co-ordinated, it will stimulate efficiency to an extent otherwise unachievable, and it will allow a degree of freedom of choice otherwise unrealisable. It works essentially by transmitting information (principally via price signals) from consumers to producers and back again.

Consumers have the power of exit from suppliers which do not suit them and so enjoy greater security of supply and lower prices than when they are in the hands of monopolists (state or other). Minorities find that their wants are met in ways which a political market-place (which serves the majority) is incapable of reproducing. Producers find that efficiency standards are automatically set for them by the actions of competitors because they cannot afford to fall behind. Thus there is a constant stimulus to innovation and entrepreneurship which promotes economic progress.

A very significant corollary of the Austrian view is that, because markets are essentially discovery mechanisms, their results cannot be reproduced by regulation, government control or similar means. *The results of competitive markets can be achieved only by the process of discovery.*

More Rules for Regulators?

This apparently simple idea yields some very significant conclusions. For instance, take the present debate in Britain (which is very relevant to the energy industries) about whether there should be more rules for regulators and whether regulators should be brought together in groups for consistency in decision-making. From an Austrian perspective, laying down more rules for utility regulators or combining regulatory bodies into one are actions at best irrelevant and indeed more likely to make regulation worse than better. Regulators can never know what the outcome of a competitive

[55]

market would have been, so providing them with tighter rules or co-ordinating the actions of one regulator with those of other regulators cannot help decision-making, though it may well make it more rigid.

Minimising Regulation

Much more important is to minimise regulation, confining it to genuine 'natural monopolies' (which are very few and far between these days and anyway tend to be eroded by changes in technology, as in telecommunications). Where regulation at present exists but the regulatee is not naturally monopolistic (such as in electricity generation), temporary pro-competition regulation is the answer, leading to the withering away of the regulatory body over time as it is replaced by a competitive market.

Such arguments for markets are a long way from the old-fashioned textbook case that there is a state which can be described as a perfectly competitive market the results of which one should aim to simulate because it produces 'socially desirable' results. The competitive market is a process, not a state. In this imperfect world, we are far better off relying principally on decentralised market discovery processes than on centralised government procedures. If we want the freedom which comes from allowing a wide range of preferences to be met and we want efficiency in providing goods and services, markets are far superior to the political system. Government is the prime (though not necessarily the sole) instrument for providing law and order and national defence, establishing and maintaining property rights, promoting and sustaining competition and – quite important in the energy field where one of our oldest-established industries has for years been in decline – for tempering the effects of decline and providing a safety net for the disadvantaged. But most governments stray far outside such bounds for the reasons already given and the reverse invisible hand acts to make matters worse, not better. Many of the services provided by the state are not so much demanded as supplied.

[56]

However, many people clearly distrust market outcomes. Economists who see markets in the static terms in which many textbooks still portray them show this distrust; moreover, economists have some self-interest in playing down the advantages of markets because government action is job-creating as far as they are concerned. Non-economists, not surprisingly, find the rather subtle case for using markets difficult to grasp. Governments, of whatever party, have an interest in promoting the advantages of intervention and most of the Press swallow this case unthinkingly.

Most of 'the second-hand dealers in ideas'[56] have accepted that central planning has failed but they have not drawn the logical conclusion – that, for essentially the same reasons that central planning failed, most government intervention will also fail. The demonstrations many years ago by von Mises and Hayek that the informational and calculational requirements of centralised planning and forecasting are such that it is very unlikely ever to be socially beneficial (though it may, of course, provide benefits to those who do the planning) apply, *mutatis mutandis*, to lesser measures of government intervention.[57]

Markets may appear impersonal, lacking an obvious guiding hand and suffering from numerous 'imperfections'. There is a strong temptation to try to improve on them – as indeed one should if the object is to stimulate competition, for example by easing entry to markets. But many people are also tempted to think that if only *they* could make the plans they could improve substantially on the market outcome.

Energy – 'Too Important to Be Left to the Market'?

That is particularly so in energy which, it is frequently remarked, is 'too important to be left to the market'. There

---

56 F.A.Hayek, 'The Intellectuals and Socialism', *University of Chicago Law Review*, Vol.16, No.3, Spring 1949.

57 See, for example, Kirzner, *op. cit.*, especially p.136.

are large numbers of would-be energy planners who would like to over-ride preferences as they appear in the market-place, imposing on others their own preferences – whether for more 'energy efficiency', for particular aspects of a cleaner environment or for protection of particular fuel industries. There is a strong authoritarian streak, in addition to self-interest, in most of the pleas for 'long-term co-ordinated' energy policies or for setting particular shares for given fuels.

What are the failures with which, it is alleged, energy markets cannot cope?[58]

Security of Supply

It is argued that government has a rôle in promoting security of supply because it has some public good aspects (not all the benefits can be appropriated by the provider). Many British government actions in the energy market have been justified on security grounds although, more often than not, security is just an excuse for actions taken for quite different reasons. In any case, the effects have been perverse. British Coal was protected for many years on 'security' grounds, *yet the main result was to promote insecurity by making British consumers of coal and electricity dependent on a single supplier of coal.*

The theoretical argument is in any case unsound. Both consumers and producers have interests in secure supplies and will naturally diversify to provide them. The main reason the market under-provides is that it is rigged by political action: suppliers know that if they anticipate and provide for emergencies they will not be allowed to appropriate the benefits (for instance, by increasing prices). Therefore they have no incentive to make provision. There may be a case for some government action to provide against emergencies (say, some excess stocking) but it tends to undermine commercial incentives for secure supplies.

---

58 For more discussion, see Eileen Marshall and Colin Robinson, *The Economics of Energy Self-Sufficiency*, London: Heinemann Educational Books, 1984, and Colin Robinson, 'Depletion Control in Theory and Practice', *Zeitschrift für Energie Wirtschaft*, 1/86, January 1986.

Balance of Payments

Balance-of-payments reasons have been invoked by British governments for protecting indigenous energy industries (mainly coal but also nuclear) against market forces. The argument is complete nonsense. It cannot improve the balance of payments, or any other indicator of economic performance to buy high-cost home-produced goods and services when cheaper imports are available.

Protection Against Rising Prices of Imported Fuels

Another common argument is that we cannot afford to become dependent on imported fuels, as a competitive market might dictate, because in the long run the prices of those fuels will rise. Since history shows that the long-run tendency of real fuel costs and prices is to decline,[59] the empirical evidence for this case is weak. Nor is the implicit case – that some clever people can foresee trends in fuel prices to which markets are blind – at all convincing. One might have thought that those who are risking their money would be better predictors than would-be planners.

There is a possible insurance-premium-type argument for support for indigenous fuels on the grounds that imported fuel prices *might* go very high in the future. But calculating the correct premium – so as to incorporate not only the probability of those higher prices but also 'society's' attitude towards risk – would be a daunting task.

Safeguarding Future Generations

Competitive markets are said to neglect the interests of future generations. For example, producers of a resource might discount the future at 'too high' a rate, leaving too little of that

---

59 A classic study by Barnett and Morse (H.J. Barnett and C. Morse, *Scarcity and Growth: The Economics of Natural Resource Scarcity*, Baltimore, MD: Johns Hopkins Press, 1963) showed that the real costs of extracting most resources in the USA, including fuels, had fallen substantially in the previous one hundred years. Subsequent studies confirm these results, despite the temporary increase in costs and prices in the 1970s. The main reason for declining costs appears to be improvements in technology.

resource in the ground for their successors. Resource markets are imperfect and will never achieve 'optimum' rates of depletion (in the Pareto sense) except by chance.

But, in all such matters, one must ask: What is the alternative? Would it have been better if, in the second half of the 18th century some resource conservationists – ahead of their time – had persuaded the British government to keep coal resources in the ground? We would have had plenty of coal now but we would have missed the discovery process which resulted from the exploitation of Britain's coal resources. Natural resources, when used, are not lost but transformed into technological advances, other new knowledge and increased use of capital.

Moreover, when considering market 'short-termism', one must remember that most participants in markets have a much longer perspective than most politicians. Compared to the alternative of political action, it is simply not true that markets take a short-term view. Clever people who believe they can form a much better long-term view than can market participants, even to the extent of perceiving how to promote the interests of future generations, should be (but evidently are not) immensely rich. If markets really are so short-sighted, anyone able to see beyond the end of his or her nose could make a killing by using that long perspective to invest.

Environmental Externalities

It is claimed that markets fail to take full account of some environmental effects because they are externalities which fall on individuals and organisations other than those taking the offending action, and that they are uncompensated or under-compensated. Although the case is for a government environmental policy rather than a government energy policy, it is necessarily linked to the energy industries because of their significant environmental impact.

The case may appear overwhelming to those who think in market-failure terms. It is less so to those who recognise the extent of government failure and observe the problems to which government action in the energy field has led. A particular difficulty is that, if there is to be a successful environmental policy run by government, that government must submerge all its short-term political interests and concentrate on achieving benefits which will accrue in the long term when the originating administration will be long gone and a different party may well be in power. It seems unlikely political behaviour. Unfortunately, it seems more probable that governments will use 'green' concerns as excuses for actions they wanted to take anyway which have little to do with genuine concern about the environment. That seems to have been the case with the fuel tax increases in Mr Lamont's last Budget in March 1993.

In general, it seems preferable to use market forces to the fullest extent possible (though opinions will differ on what that extent is) rather than to rely on political action. The politicisation of environmental matters will bring a short-term perspective to environmental affairs and deliver excessive regulation by people who can impose costs confident that they will always fall on others. For that reason a greater effort is required to find market solutions to environmental problems, whether 'global' or local. As with security of supply issues, the reason why markets do not work well in environmental matters is often because they are not allowed to do so – in particular, because property rights are not always clearly enough defined so that owners can defend their property against damage by polluters as against others.[60] The main problems reside in so-called 'global' effects where scientific knowledge is very poor and which are not so obviously amenable to property rights solutions.

6. Summary and Conclusions

BRITISH ENERGY 'POLICY' has a poor record extending back over many years. Until very recently, there was an increasingly protectionist trend because policy was dominated by producer pressure groups which took advantage of the desire of

---

60 Terry L. Anderson and Donald R. Leal, *Free Market Environmentalism*, San Francisco: Pacific Research Institute, 1991.

politicians to capture votes. Privatisation has to some extent reduced government activity in energy markets. Nevertheless, the privatisation schemes themselves were heavily influenced by the wishes of the producer groups concerned which had interests in common with governments anxious to raise substantial revenues and to widen share ownership. The consequence was limited liberalisation of product markets. Liberalisation was left mainly to industry regulators and the competition authorities, delaying the benefits of competition and, given the power of the incumbents, leading to awkward regulatory problems.

This *Occasional Paper* has emphasised the advantages of competitive markets as well as the disadvantages of government action. In the light of these advantages and disadvantages, a policy specifically for energy seems not only unnecessary but undesirable. Whatever excuses are given, in practice 'policy' has generally arisen from pursuit of short-term political interests, supported by the producer pressure groups which thrive and lobby government whenever a market is seen to be politicised. In such markets short-termism and excessive lobbying are inherent. Adjustment processes are hampered and participants in the market are induced to invest resources in influencing government rather than in trying to improve the efficiency of their activities.

In energy markets, as elsewhere, there is no sense in recommending policies, based on supposed 'imperfections' and 'failures' in markets, which would be unlikely to work even if we were governed by far-sighted saints and angels. Given the world in which we live, if the aims are increasing efficiency, the prevalence of long-term views and representation of the interests of consumers, the best (though 'imperfect') answer is to rely primarily on energy markets. Attempts by politicians and civil servants, no matter how well-meaning they may be, to provide policies for energy are much more likely to be a hindrance than a help.

IEA TITLES ALREADY PUBLISHED IN 1993

All prices include postage and packing.

Should the Taxpayer Support the Arts?

DAVID SAWERS

1. No substantial subsidy to the arts in Britain is either necessary or desirable.

2. Subsidy is unnecessary because the British cultural heritage was created without the aid of governments, when incomes were a fraction of present levels; now people are much richer and better educated, the arts can flourish without government support.

3. Subsidy is undesirable because the people who benefit from it are likely to be richer than those who pay for it, and because it allows governments and government agencies to influence the development of the arts.

4. Any future subsidies should help to preserve the cultural heritage, promote knowledge of the arts among the young, and meet local demands. Tax relief for gifts to artistic charities should be retained.

5. Museums should continue to receive a reduced subsidy, but their collections should be dispersed more evenly around the country.

6. Teaching about the arts should be promoted in schools; students could be given subsidised access to the performing arts and museums.

7. Local authorities should be free to subsidise the arts in their area, employing locally raised revenue, if their electorate so desires. The beneficiaries of local subsidies are more likely to be the same as the financiers than with national subsidies.

8. Funds from the national lottery should not be used to support the arts; its supporters are likely to be poorer than the average taxpayer, so this use would be especially inequitable.

9. Future aid to the arts should be administered by the Department for Education, which can best judge priorities between work on the arts in schools, museums, and subsidising attendance at performances. The Department of National Heritage and the Arts Council should be abolished.

10. The development of the arts should be left to individuals; the main role of the state should be that of educator rather than subsidiser.

ISBN 0-255 36325-7   Current Controversies No.7

The Institute of Economic Affairs
2 Lord North Street, Westminster
London SW1P 3LB
Telephone: 071-799 3745

£3.95